Faith to Move Mountains
Stirring our Faith to Believe for Movements among the Unreached, Digital Edition
Based on Print Edition
Copyright 2017 by K Sutter, C Anderson
All rights reserved.
Scripture quotations are taken from THE HOLY BIBLE, NEW INTERNATIONAL VERSION
Copyright 1973, 1978, 1984 International Bible Society.
Printed in the United States of America

Forward

This book was originally written in a paperback format to encourage indigenous church planters in Asia to believe God for multiplying movements of disciples. In the past six years since it was first written, we have seen a significant change in Asia and many, many groups of Jesus followers have been started among unreached peoples! Supernatural Increase has begun! Some places where there had only been a handful of believers, now have hundreds or even thousands. Multi-generational growth has taken off in many villages, towns and cities. Movements are happening! In many more places, the discipleship groups are about to shift into multiplicative growth. It is our prayer that where you work and minister will be one of those places as well!

Two years after it was written, a companion guide written for intercessors and prayer partners was also created. That guide contains prayer points and some additional information helpful to those who are not as familiar with missions terminologies.

With the release of this e-book version, we hope many will be encouraged to believe God for greater fruit and a tremendous harvest! Believing it is possible and something God wants to do is the first step. As you read and pray through these short devotionals, may fresh faith stir in your heart for what God wants to do.

Introduction:

Two versions of this devotional are available: one for cross-cultural workers spreading the Good News on the "frontlines" and one for those standing with them and praying for them from the "home-front."

The Great Commandment, love God & love your neighbor as yourself and The Great Commission, spread that love to the ends of the earth—were given for all believers to joyfully obey. Together we cooperate in getting the Good News of Jesus Christ to the remaining unreached tongues, tribes and nations—those who have never heard. Some of us work out on the frontiers of the Gospel and some of us work from our hometowns. If we are to see God's Kingdom come and His will done in today's hurting world, we need "faith to move mountains." Here is a way for you meditate upon Bible stories and truths relevant to this great task. You will be stirred to consider ways to apply them in your personal life. You will also be helped to pray in a focused manner for frontline workers to apply these truths in their lives and within their ministries.

Our workers on the frontlines of the Gospel's advance need inspiration and prayer. The Apostle Paul, one of the greatest pioneer missionaries urged the church to pray for him, "...keep alert with all perseverance, making supplication for all the saints, and also for me, that words may be given to me in opening my mouth boldly to proclaim the mystery of the Gospel, for which I am an ambassador in chains, that I may declare it boldly, as I ought to speak." Ephesians 6:19-20 Paul knew he needed the church to understand what he was doing and with that understanding, to pray in faith. All frontline workers need this kind of prayer.

A few weeks ago I received a letter from my friend Goutam. He serves cross-culturally in North India. His plea to me and his other friends: "Devote yourselves to prayer, being watchful and thankful. And pray for us, too, that God may open a door for our message, so that we may proclaim the mystery of Christ...." (Colossians 4:2-3) I understand what Goutam is seeking to accomplish and I pray in faith he will succeed!

May this little book build you up in faith for God's work in your own life. May it also further equip you for prayer, a major role in the completion of the Great Commission.

Until All Have Heard,
K. Sutter

A Word from K. Sutter

A conviction grew and grew within me - God wants to unite us in a fresh way around His Kingdom purposes. Something great is coming. I felt I was supposed to present this to the Global Leadership Team of Youth With A Mission. This was a bit intimidating so I needed to be sure. With all sincerity, I took this before the Lord asking Him to confirm it.

Living near the ocean, I found a place overlooking the water and began to pray. In my journal I wrote my prayer, "I'm feeling insecure—I don't want to be overly confident—'I've got the Word of the Lord!' So I yield to You— Lord and King. Lord of the Harvest, please speak."

Immediately I sensed He was directing me to notice the tide. The tide was low but I could not tell if the tide was coming in or still going out. The Lord spoke, "There is a constant ebb and flow. To really know what's happening you have to watch. Watch. Observe. Focus on what I'm doing."

As I sat observing, it occurred to me that I had a way to know what the tide was doing. Because I am a surfer, I carry a small "tide chart" in my pocket. It helps me choose a good day and time to go surfing. I pulled out the chart and looked for the date, July 10, 2007. The chart listed low tide at 2:13pm. I looked at my watch: it displayed 2:13pm. I was so shocked, I nearly fell off the bench!

I wrote in my journal what I believe the Lord said, "Well now you know that the tide has just turned. I am bringing in the water. The tide is rising. I am bringing something Good. My goodness and My love will be seen by many!"

The tide has turned. The tide of God's blessings to the nations is rising.

A few months later on Jeju Island, South Korea, I presented this "word" to the Global Leadership Team of Youth With A Mission. They embraced it and responded in faith.

In 2010, God spoke to our leaders in South Asia to believe Him and work with Him for supernatural increase. I easily embraced this in faith. I recognized it as part of what He spoke to me. He is calling us all to join with Him in His work. Let's respond to Jesus in obedience and faith. This booklet is intended to inspire us through Biblical examples of obedience and faith. Read it, meditate upon God's Word, respond to the challenging questions and pray for the frontline workers serving among unreached people groups.

A Word from C. Anderson

Like K. Sutter, I believe that we are in an unusual time in history. Things are changing. God is accelerating (speeding up) his work in the world and bringing in a great harvest. I want to be a part of that! In early 2010, while on a prayer retreat I asked God to speak to me. I was in a new role and had taken a new responsibility of leadership in our mission. I deeply longed to hear His voice. What would He say to me at this time? What Word or direction would He give? My heart was hungry and the Shepherd so faithfully spoke during those days away.

God showed me that He wanted to bring about a great increase in our fruitfulness. He wanted and expected us to increase. He wanted us to believe Him for more...much more...than we had seen Him already do among the unreached!

It is my prayer that this book will inspire both frontline workers and those who stand with them in prayer. Let us believe Him for more! We serve a great God. Nothing is too hard for Him. We can do the impossible as we are yoked to Him, as we join Him in what He is doing among the unreached.

A Prayer as We Begin this Book:

Lord, please grant us the faith that moves mountains. Help us in prayer to stand alongside Your workers in the Harvest and trust You for supernatural increase. Our hope is in You. Amen.

DAY 1

Supernatural Increase

by C. Anderson

Luke 19:16-17 *"The first one came and said, 'Sir, your mina has earned ten more.' 'Well done, my good servant,' his master replied...."*

The master went away to receive his kingdom. Before going he gave one mina, or coin, to ten of his servants. Each was given the instruction "Put this money to work until I come back." When the master returned he called his servants to him. The first servant came and reported to the master that his one mina had now become 10. He received the praise of the master and was given responsibility for 10 cities.

The second servant reported a five-fold increase. His one coin had become five. He too was given more responsibility and authority by the master. The third servant though, had buried what he had been given and it had remained the same. He had neither grown what he had been given nor put it to work as the master had said to do. This servant was called a wicked servant and removed from the kingdom.

This well known parable speaks to us of God's expectation that His followers would take what they have been given and increase it. God expects us to grow! He expects us to multiply! And He expects us to multiply a lot!

What would it look like in our work among Muslims, Hindus and Buddhists if we saw an increase of 10 times in the next few years? What if 20 believers became 200? Or 3 house churches became 30 house churches? Let's ask God for this kind of supernatural growth. He is able and He can do this through us!

One day we will hear Him say "Well done, faithful servant. You've taken what I've given you - multiplied it and increased it!"

Personal questions to consider:

1. How are you investing what God has given you to see an increase of His Kingdom?
2. In what ways may you be focused on what you don't have, rather than using and increasing what you do have in your hands already?

Pray for the Frontline Workers to:

1. Receive ever-increasing levels of faith.
2. Recognize what would need to change in their hearts to believe God for a 10-times increase in fruitfulness in the harvest.

Your thoughts:

Multiplied Bread and Fish

by K. Sutter

John 6:5-7 *"When Jesus looked up and saw a great crowd coming toward Him, He said to Philip, "Where shall we buy bread for these people to eat?" He asked this only to test him, for He already had in mind what He was going to do. Philip answered Him, 'It would take more than half a year's wages to buy enough bread for each one to have a bite!'"*

Facing a great crowd of hungry people in a remote place, Jesus turned to Philip and asks a question that stretches his faith. From Philip's perspective, buying enough bread for all these people was impossible. No way.

Yesterday's devotional challenged us to believe for a ten-fold increase in fruit over the next few years. For many of our frontline workers, a 10-fold increase is impossible. But if indeed the Lord has given us this challenge, we can expect "He already has in mind what He is going to do."

Jesus had a plan. He would do His part, others would do theirs. The disciples had no food to contribute, but rather than throw up their hands in frustration at Jesus' wild request, they took action. Andrew, found a local boy. 'Here is a boy with five small barley loaves and two small fish....' At least this was something—all that was humanly possible. Comparing this little bit of bread and sh to what was needed, Andrew asked: "....but how far will they go among so many?'"

Jesus took the small loaves and fish, gave thanks to God and began giving, giving and giving. Everyone was well fed. A miracle took place, the goal was reached. All the people were amazed by Jesus. "Surely, He is the Prophet we have been expecting!"

Many of us are asking God for a 10-fold increase in the harvest. Without God it is impossible. But He can multiply. One of our church planting teams working in an unreached Asian city saw the number of their disciples grow from 14 to 120 in one year and to 240 the next year, and God used local young people who offered the little they had to Jesus. Let Jesus stretch our faith. Look beyond the natural to the supernatural. Let us bring to Jesus what we currently have and ask Him to multiply it. If He lifts it up and blesses it, multiplication will come.

So amazing was the feeding of the 5,000 that the story is told in all four gospels. Jesus has not stopped doing amazing things. May He use us in creating new stories that spread His fame!

Personal questions to consider:

1. What fruit do you currently have from your service for Jesus? How will you thank Him?
2. What would multiplication of this fruit look like?

Pray for the Frontline Workers to:

1. Celebrate the fruit they already have from their work and chose how they will offer it to Jesus so He can bless and multiply it.
2. Discern which local people might join with them like the boy in the story. To recognize what local resources they can bring, like the five loaves and two fish.

Your thoughts:

DAY 3

Be Strong and Courageous

by C. Anderson

Joshua 1:9   *"Have I not commanded you? Be strong and courageous. Do not be terrified; do not be discouraged, for the LORD your God will be with you wherever you go."*

In the first chapter of Joshua, the words "Be strong and courageous" are repeated four different times! God was trying to get a message through to this new leader. Moses was dead and now it was Joshua's time to rise up and lead the people. It was his season. It was his destiny. It was what God had prepared him for. Yet, he was afraid. He would face many difficulties and many challenges ahead. There were battles to be fought, rivers to cross, and enemies to push back. He was going into new territory, taking new land. Joshua must have needed to hear those words more than just once.

As church planters work in the frontiers they are much like Joshua. They are taking new places and peoples for His Kingdom. They are going into new territory and pushing back the forces of darkness. Sometimes they feel young and inexperienced. Yet, like Joshua, they are the ones God has chosen for this task.

When He calls any of us He promises to be with us, to go before us, to fight for us and to help us in every situation. He speaks to us all today, once again, "Be strong and courageous. Be strong and courageous. Be strong and courageous. Be strong and very courageous."

This strength is not just a physical strength. It is a strength of spirit, a strength of heart. God spoke to Joshua and he speaks to us, "Don't give in to fear and doubt. Be strong in your spirit. Rise up in faith and the power of God. Be courageous!" Courage is the quality of mind or spirit that enables a person to face difficulty, danger or pain... without fear. To be courageous means to look at those dangers, fears or difficulties and to say "I refuse to let you control me. I'm going forward in spite of you!" This strength and courage comes from the sure knowledge that God is with us. If God is for us, then who can be against us? We have no reason to fear.

God had promised the Israelites the land long before they entered. Joshua was taking them in to take possession. He went forward based on the command and promise of God. As we work among unreached peoples, we must remember these two things. God has promised to give us these people. It's already written in the Book of Revelation that people from every tribe and nation will worship Him. God has commanded His disciples to go to all nations and peoples with His Good News. So we will rise up and be strong.

We will face the dangers and difficulties with courage. We will cross our Jordans and take possession of the people groups he has given us. For we know our God is with us!

Personal questions to consider:

1. How strong do you feel in your spirit today? Speak to your soul with the Scripture above.
2. What are you facing now that requires courage? What will you do next?

Pray for the Frontline Workers to:

1. Find strength for their spirits from God and His word.
2. Identify what difficulty, danger or pain is trying to keep them afraid to go forward or to keep working for God.

Your thoughts:

_____
_____
_____
_____
_____
_____
_____
_____
_____
_____
_____
_____

Fear Paralyzes

by K. Sutter

Matt 14:28-29   *"'Lord, if it's You,' Peter replied, 'tell me to come to You on the water.' 'Come,' He said."*

The disciples were filled with fear when they first saw Jesus walking toward their wave-tossed boat late at night. "Take heart; it is I. Do not be afraid," was His response. Peter was still uncertain, but he tried to take heart. He gathered his courage and got out of the boat when he heard Jesus say "Come." Step by step he walked upon the water, making his way toward Jesus. Suddenly the frightening circumstances got the best of him. Again he was afraid. He began to sink.

Fear caused Peter to sink. Fear also causes us to sink. When we sink in fear, we become unfruitful. In Matthew 25:14-30 Jesus told the story of two good and faithful servants and then a third servant who sank in fear. In fact, he sank his master's gold in the ground. His excuse to his angry master: "So I was afraid and went out and hid your gold in the ground." His master called him wicked.

Beware of fear. In a letter I received this week, a South Asian worker serving in Central Asia wrote, "Over the last couple of years, I have learned that the Taliban, Al Qaeda and Islamic governments are not our enemies, but we ourselves are our own enemy. Our fear and anxiety paralyze us and keep us from doing God's will." Fear paralyzes.

Fear causes us to sink, but faith always lifts us up. As Peter began to sink, he cried out, "Lord, save me!" Jesus immediately reached out His hand and took hold of him. Together, Jesus and Peter hand-in-hand walked to the boat.

It seems I've always focused upon the fact that Peter began to sink—he gave into fear and failed. But that is not the end of the story. In the end, he turned from fear and cried out to Jesus. Peter won, fear lost! Well done good and faithful Peter!
"Come" Jesus says to us, "Walk with Me into the impossible." In spite of the challenge of making disciples among unreached peoples, cross-cultural workers have stepped out of their homes and away from their families and cultures to walk with Jesus.

When those times come, as they will, when surrounding circumstances bring fear, remember Jesus' words, "Take heart. It is I. Do not be afraid." Do not let fear pull you down. Let faith in Jesus lift you up. Grab His outstretched hand and walk on with Him.

Personal questions to consider:

1. What "impossibilities" do you see in your life that are similar to Peter's attempt to walk on water?
2. When was the last time you faced fear but then cried out to Jesus? What was the outcome?

Pray for the Frontline Workers to:

1. Identify "impossibilities" they see in their church planting ministry that are similar to Peter's attempt to walk on water.
2. Recall the last time they faced a fearful situation and cried out to Jesus. To be encouraged as they remember His help.

Your thoughts:

_____

_____

_____

_____

_____

_____

_____

_____

_____

_____

_____

_____

Faith Overpowers Fear

by K. Sutter

Matthew 14:32-33 *"And when they climbed into the boat, the wind died down. Then those who were in the boat worshiped Him, saying, 'Truly You are the Son of God.'"*

Peter and Jesus, hand-in-hand walked upon the water . They climbed into the boat as the wind howled and waves slammed against the hull. Peter overcame fear by placing all his faith in Jesus. Perhaps his faith inspired the rest of the disciples. Suddenly the disciples' faith overpowered their fear and worship arose. The fruit of faith was worship. The fruit of worship was revelation: "Truly You are the Son of God."

Faith creates fruit. Fear kills fruit. Jesus explained this in the parable of The Sower and the Seed. "The seed falling among the thorns refers to someone who hears the Word, but the worries of this life…choke the Word, making it unfruitful." (Matthew 13:22) Worries and fears are like thorns threatening to encircle and destroy. These thorns are only overpowered by faith. Though fear may come, faith will overcome.

A church planting team in the Philippines could have been choked by fear and their work destroyed. They had chosen a poor, crime-ridden community for their evangelistic Bible stories. This was the place where many unreached tribal people settled as they came from the surrounding mountains. The team knew the dangers but believed God wanted to bring transformation to the people and their community.

One terrible morning a young married couple was unusually late to the team meeting. Two coworkers were sent to their house to remind them of the meeting. Something was wrong—there was blood at the doorway. Opening the door, they discovered the couple brutally murdered. Shock, horror, sorrow, mourning, pain and defeat were only a fraction of what they all faced through this intense storm.

Like Peter, they cried to Jesus. Before long, YWAMers and churches across the world cried out too. This church planting team chose not to allow fear to paralyze. Taking Jesus by the hand, the team walked through a time of healing. Eventually, two members of the team agreed to go back into the community and re-start the Bible stories. As they walked down the road, one turned to the other saying, "I'm afraid." His friend answered, "Me too." Yet they continued walking.

Melchor, a young tribal man watched with surprise from a distance. Until now, he had been resisting the message of the Gospel. "What courage. What faith." he thought. Their example penetrated his heart and he too reached out to Jesus. In the years ahead, Melchor became a wonderfully fruitful, pioneer church planter among an unreached tribe. Once as I visited him in the rice-terraced mountains, Melchor joyfully told me of the day he baptized 50 families in a river.

Overcoming worry and fear is a key to bearing supernatural fruit even "a crop, yielding a hundred, sixty or thirty times what was sown." (Matt 13:23)

Personal questions to consider:

1. There are "worries of this life." What are your worries?
2. In Matthew 6:25-34, Jesus commands three times, "Do not worry…do not worry…do not worry…." What do you do to obey His command to not worry?

Pray for the Frontline Workers to:

1. List any "worries of life" which are troubling them.
2. Obey Jesus, stop worrying and bring their burdens to Him. That their example of faith will inspire those who see their lives.

Your thoughts:

DAY 6

Delight in His Law

by C. Anderson

Ps. 1:2-3   *"But his delight is in the law of the Lord, and on his law he meditates day and night. He is like a tree planted by streams of water which yields its fruit in season and whose leaf does not wither, whatever he does prospers."*

What is the greatest key to fruitfulness in church planting? What is needed if we truly want to see thousands of people coming to know the Lord and many hundreds of house churches planted? This passage in Psalms says that the person who delights in the Law of God, and who meditates on God's Word will yield much fruit in season. It says that whatever that person does will prosper. For our frontline workers, it means they will see the multiplication of disciples and churches... supernatural increase... because church planting is what they do!

It is easy for busy church planters to get their focus on the work and off of God. If this happens, they read the Bible only to prepare stories or to prepare for discipleship times. Time alone with God takes second place, with ministry coming first. The pressures are great. People come to their houses all hours of the day and night, their phone is constantly ringing with this problem or that.

The person who delights in God's Word and meditates on it will see fruitfulness. They will not be burned out and exhausted by the strain of the constant demands. Their roots will go down deep and be planted in the steams of water so their soul will be refreshed in God. Out of this abundance and spiritual health comes the fruit of many people knowing and receiving Jesus.

Let's all commit ourselves to be students of the Word of God, to meditate on it daily, to delight in spending time allowing God's Word to speak deeply into our hearts. And let's believe God for increase and growth in our fruitfulness.

Personal questions to consider:

1. How often do you meditate on God's Word? What helps you to think about it and allow it to speak to your heart?
2. What will help you grow in the spiritual discipline of Bible Study and Scripture meditation this week?

Pray for the Frontline Workers to:

1. Not allow busyness to draw them away from quality time with God. To faithfully meditate upon His Word and allow it to speak to their hearts.
2. Effectively teach their disciples to love the Word of God and meditate upon it daily.

Your thoughts:

_____

_____

_____

_____

_____

_____

_____

_____

_____

_____

_____

_____

_____

_____

Levi Transformed

by K. Sutter

Luke 5:27-29   *"'Follow Me,' Jesus said to him, and Levi got up, left everything and followed Him."*

Levi heard Jesus' words and looked into Jesus' face. Now nothing else in his life mattered. He got up from his tax booth and followed Jesus. Jesus captured Levi's attention then captured his heart. The encounter was so overwhelmingly wonderful that Levi made Jesus a great feast and brought his fellow tax collectors and friends to join the celebration.

This is the impact Jesus has upon those who meet Him. He's done this with millions of people like Levi for 2,000 years. He is still doing it today and will do it tomorrow.

One of our church planters who worked in Mongolia tells of a Mongol man who met Jesus one morning. He was urged by the church planter to immediately go share his faith. Joyfully, home he went to tell his family. Before long he went to the neighbors on the right side of his house. He went to the neighbors on the left side of his house. By the end of the day, 24 people met Jesus! A new fellowship began in his home.

Let's stir our faith. Let's believe that the people we reach out to will "hear" His voice and "see" His face. Let's have faith that He will impact them as He did Levi-- capturing their attention and capturing their hearts. Let's believe they will be transformed by Jesus' love and power and then freely tell family and friends.

Levi (also called Matthew) was transformed. Once a despised collector of Roman taxes, he became one of The Twelve and the author of the Gospel of Matthew, said to be the most widely read book in the world!

Personal questions to consider:

1. Who are three people you know who were dramatically transformed by Jesus?
2. Who are three people you will pray for to meet Jesus in similar ways?

Pray for the Frontline Workers to:

1. Choose specific unreached people to pray for diligently.
2. Build up their faith to believe these and others will hear, see and follow Jesus.

Your thoughts:

_____

_____

_____

_____

_____

_____

_____

_____

_____

_____

_____

_____

_____

_____

With Eyes of Faith

by C. Anderson

1 Samuel 17:45-47   *David said to the Philistine "You come against me with sword and spear and javelin, but I come against you in the Name of the LORD Almighty, the God of the armies of Israel, whom you have defied. This day the Lord will hand you over to me…All will know..that it is not by sword or spear that the Lord saves; for the battle is the LORD's and he will give all of you into our hands."*

David saw his enemy with eyes of faith. The Israelite army looked at Goliath and saw his great size and his great spear. They were scared by his threats. David was not intimidated. He saw God's power! He knew that the power of the Name of the LORD Almighty was greater than any enemy.

David saw himself with eyes of faith. His brothers thought he was too young, that he was just a boy. How could he think someone as young and inexperienced as he, could fight against this giant? They questioned his motives and said he was proud. David was not proud, but he was confident in the power of God to do the impossible.

David took actions of faith. He chose not to run, but to enter the battle. He chose not to hide or run away from the opposition he faced. He stepped forward in faith and confidence. He took a great risk.

God is looking for Davids today. He is looking for people who will rise up in faith to stand against the giants. When we look at the task of reaching the unreached and planting churches in new places, it can seem so difficult. Sometimes we are intimidated or scared when we see the spiritual forces, or strongholds that are ruling over the people or places we are trying to reach. It is easy to become intimidated by the enemy rather than confident in God and His great power to save and deliver.

Don't allow yourself to be more impressed with the giants in the land, than you are with the power of God! The MIGHTY ONE OF ISRAEL is with you today! He is powerful to save…powerful to deliver…and He lives in you! The battle is the Lord's, and you come against the enemy in His Name! Believe God today for breakthroughs and victory.

Believe Him today for giants to fall and new people to come to know Jesus. Believe Him today for that movement of thousands of transformed lives and new followers of our Lord.

Personal questions to consider:

1. When are you more intimidated or impressed by the enemy's power than God's power?
2. In what ways do you look at your situations with eyes of faith?

Pray for the Frontline Workers to:

1. Become aware of times they are more intimidated or impressed by the enemy's power than God's power.
2. Find ways to boldly step out in aggressive faith to confront the strongholds in the land.

Your thoughts:

_____
_____
_____
_____
_____
_____
_____
_____
_____
_____
_____
_____
_____

Simple Messengers and Simple Ways

by C. Anderson

2 Kings 5:15   *"Then Naaman and all his attendants went back to the man of God. He stood before him and said, "Now I know that there is no God in all the world except in Israel."*

Naaman was a hero of his people. He was highly regarded and a great commander. But he had a problem. He had leprosy. Everyone has some kind of problem. There isn't a person on earth who doesn't have some kind of felt need. Naaman's need was for healing. A little servant girl saw that need and pointed him in the right direction.

She told her mistress of a prophet in Samaria that she was sure could heal her master. What faith! What confidence she must have had to share this so that they believed and took action. This little girl had been taken away from her family. She was a captive and a slave. Yet she allowed God to use her to share good news with her oppressors. And they listened!

Naaman went to see Elisha. When he got there, Elisha didn't go out to meet him. He simply sent a message. Naaman should go and wash himself seven times in the Jordan and he would be healed. Naaman was offended! The prophet hadn't done what he expected. He should have come and laid hands on him and called on the name of his God! This isn't the way God works, he thought. This is far too simple! After his servants encouraged him though, he obeyed. He found that God's way worked, not matter how simple it sounded. Amazed, he declared that he now knew that there was no other God but the God of Israel.

God used an unexpected messenger- a servant girl. God used an unexpected and simple method- seven dips in the river Jordan. Naaman's felt need was met, and he found the One True God. Sometimes our frontline workers feel like unlikely messengers trying to speak to great commanders. The Lord wants to use them to bring His message to the unreached. Sometimes the methods used, like storytelling and simple house churches, seem almost too simple. God's ways don't have to be complex. He uses simple ways and simple people who will simply obey … to bring about His supernatural fruit. If we watch for felt needs, if we obey Him, if we speak out His truth in faith, we will even see people of influence and status declaring "Jesus is the One True God!"

Personal questions to consider:

1. Which of God's ways and methods do you sometimes question?
2. What examples can you think of in your experience, where God has used simple people or those of low status to minister to those of influence and power?

Pray for the Frontline Workers to:

1. Not overlook the use of simple methods used by Jesus, the Apostles and the early Church.
2. Consider ways to address the felt needs of people in their community who have status and influence.

Your thoughts:

DAY 10

Recognizing Jesus

by K. Sutter

Mark 6:49-50 *"Take courage! It is I. Don't be afraid." Then He climbed into the boat with them, and the wind died down. They were completely amazed, for they had not understood about the loaves; their hearts were hardened."*

It was a rough night as the disciples struggled to keep their boat moving against strong winds. They were tired after straining at the oars. Suddenly, with weary eyes, they saw a man walking toward them on the lake and cried out in fear. "A ghost!"

Jesus said "Take courage! It is I!" He climbed into the boat with them as they sat stunned, wondering what was going on. According to Scripture, they were shocked because they failed to understand the meaning of an earlier supernatural experience with the multiplication of the loaves. What Jesus had done with the loaves had not penetrated their hearts. Their hearts and minds were callous, dull and unable to understand what was happening.

What was the meaning of the multiplication of loaves and fish? What was the miracle supposed to teach? What did the disciples miss? How would this understanding have prepared them for this new supernatural experience—Jesus walking on water? If we gain a better understanding of the miracle of the feeding of the 5,000, perhaps we also would be prepared for more of Jesus' supernatural work.

"What is He doing?" is the wrong question. "Who is doing this?" is the right question. Who He is—this is the message behind what He does. Understand who Jesus is. He wanted them to understand—to learn the truth about who He is. Only after seeing and hearing over and over did they finally understand. Later Jesus could ask, "Who do you say I am?" Peter knew, "You are the Christ." (Mark 8:29)

This is the One with Whom you and I walk. This is the One with Whom we work. This is the One of Whom it is written, "He is the radiance of the glory of God and the exact imprint of His nature, and He upholds the universe by the Word of His power." (Hebrews 1:3) "The Son is the image of the invisible God, the firstborn over all creation. For in Him all things were created: things in heaven and on earth, visible and invisible, whether thrones or powers or rulers or authorities; all things have been created through Him and for Him. He is before all things, and in Him all things hold together." (Col. 1:15-17)

He is the One worthy of our utter faith, trust, and joyful devotion. Whether we walk through a crowd of needy people or walk into the face of a storm, Jesus walks too. To those He commissioned to go make disciples of all nations, He promised, "And surely I am with you always...."

Do we recognize who it is that lifted the loaves and brought supernatural multiplication? Do we recognize who it is walking with us...even if He must walk on water? Such understanding brings courage, it is Jesus.

Personal questions to consider:

1. What helps you continue growing in your understanding of who Jesus is?
2. Where do you recognize Jesus at work now? What do you long to see Him do?

Pray for the Frontline Workers to:

1. Continue growing in their understanding of who Jesus is and help their disciples to grow as well.
2. See where Jesus is at work. Clarify their vision for reaching their people group and trust God to make it a reality.

Your thoughts:

_____
_____
_____
_____
_____
_____
_____
_____
_____
_____
_____
_____

DAY 11

Greater Things

by C. Anderson

John 14:12-13   *"I tell you the truth, anyone who has faith in Me will do what I have been doing. He will do even greater things than these, because I am going to the Father. And I will do whatever you ask in My Name, so that the Son may bring glory to the Father."*

Have you ever read these verses and thought to yourself: "This is really hard to believe. How could I possibly do greater things than Jesus did?" These are some of the most outrageous verses in the Bible. Yet they are words that Jesus actually said. He meant them!

What could those "greater things" be? Jesus healed the sick, delivered the demon possessed, gave sight to the blind, and raised the dead. As we look around the world today, we see that these miraculous signs are happening. Stories are told from Africa, South America and Asia of blind seeing, demons cast out, and even of people coming back to life. These are signs that the kingdom of God is coming here on earth.

But these signs are the same things that Jesus did, not greater things. So what are the greater things? In Jesus' own lifetime He had many followers, especially when He was giving out bread. We read of crowds of people following Him. In His three years of ministry though, Jesus did not see the transformation of the city of Jerusalem, or of the Jewish people group. During those years He didn't see thousands of groups of followers meet and join together to obey His commands. No, but this is something that we are beginning to see in the world today. We are seeing communities, cities and people groups transformed by the power of the Gospel. We are seeing hundreds of thousands of individual lives being radically changed by the message and power of Jesus!

God desires to do this even more. He longs for people from every tribe, language and people, to know Him and experience His transforming power in their communities. Could seeing hundreds of people group movements that transform their societies, be part of what Jesus meant in this verse?

Jesus said, "whatever you ask in My Name," He would do. Let's ask Him for movements…for thousands of new disciples among the unreached. Let's ask Him for breakthroughs that bring transformation. Boldly ask for unreached people groups in His Name today. He said He would do whatever you ask.

Personal questions to consider:

1. What are you asking Jesus to do as you pray in His Name?
2. Which unreached people group(s) do you pray for regularly? How involved are you in interceding for them?

Pray for the Frontline Workers to:

1. Evaluate the amount of time spent in intercession for the people group or area they are called to reach.
2. Consider how they would rank their faith level in believing God can do "greater things" through them and their team.

Your thoughts:

_____

_____

_____

_____

_____

_____

_____

_____

_____

_____

_____

_____

_____

DAY 12

The Great Intake

by K. Sutter

John 15:5-8 *"I am the vine; you are the branches. If you remain in Me and I in you, you will bear much fruit; apart from Me you can do nothing. ...If you remain in Me and My words remain in you, ask whatever you wish, and it will be done for you. This is to my Father's glory, that you bear much fruit, showing yourselves to be My disciples."*

A supernatural increase in fruit will only come from a "supernatural lifestyle." Ongoing spiritual life comes as we remain connected to Jesus, the Source of Life. First priority then, is to know God. Only as we know Him and keep growing in our knowledge and experience with Him are we equipped to make Him known to others. Pursue God, fruit will come. If we begin pursuing fruit (ministry results) apart from pursuing Him—Jesus warns us—we will accomplish nothing. He didn't say we would accomplish less—He said we would accomplish NOTHING.

In 1907 E. Stanley Jones was sent as a missionary to India. He began work among the lowest castes. In time, the Lord led him to also conducted thousands of meetings among more educated groups as well. Looking at the fruit of his 30 years in that country, many call him the "Billy Graham of India." E. Stanley Jones knew the importance of remaining connected to Jesus. He wrote "...there is one responsibility and only one responsibility—to keep in union with God. When that union with God is intact, everything flows from it. I know of no one thing that cultivates union with God more surely and constantly than the regular practice of the Quiet Time." He called his regular time alone with God "the Great Intake."

Without a "Great Intake" of Life from Jesus, our Vine, we wither into dry, dead branches. We bear no lasting fruit. But you and I are called to live a supernatural lifestyle, enjoying the steady flow from the Vine, listening to His voice and doing what He says. The result is we will bear fruit. We will bear much fruit.

Personal questions to consider:

1. In what ways do you keep yourself vitally connected to Jesus?
2. How often each week do you take time alone with Him in prayer?

Pray for the Frontline Workers to:

1. Reflect upon their level of intimacy with Jesus.
2. Realize a supernatural increase of fruit in the harvest may require an increase in time with Jesus—listening to Him and doing what He says. Pray they ask Jesus about how frequently and how much time to invest in their Quiet Times.

Your thoughts:

DAY 13

Arise! This is the Day!

by C. Anderson

Judges 4:14   *"And Deborah said to Barak, "Arise! For this is the day in which the LORD has given Sisera into your hands; behold, the LORD has gone out before you."*

The story of Deborah and Barak is an inspiring one. The Midianites had oppressed Israel for 20 years. Deborah was a prophetess, a wife and mother, and a judge. She heard the Word of the Lord and spoke it out to Barak. God said to go and fight against Midian. Barak refused to go unless Deborah joined him. She agreed, and together this two person team gathered the armies.

Then the day came. It was time. "Arise!" she says. "This is the day!" she proclaims. "The Lord has gone out before you!"

God is raising up Deborahs and Baraks today. God is looking for people who hear His voice saying "Now is the time…rise up!" Sometimes we, as well as our coworkers on the frontlines, become sleepy in our ministry or church planting work. We go about our programs, we visit our contacts, we run our fellowships. But we have lost our passion, our sense of urgency. We no longer cry out to God to see a miraculous increase and thousands of people coming to know Jesus in our area or people group. We wonder if a church planting movement is even possible. God would say to us all today "Wake up! Rise up! I am with you! I have gone before you!"

Not all of the tribes of Israel joined Deborah and Barak. Some stayed back and missed out on the battle, and on the victory. God is calling us forward. Let's not hold back, but believe that God is with us and victory is sure! A church planting movement is on the way. The Lord has gone out before you.

Personal questions to consider:

1. Barak needed Deborah beside him to encourage his faith. Who do you have in your life to inspire you with faith and courage?
2. How can you be a "Deborah" to someone else?

Pray for the Frontline Workers to:

1. Inspire their teammates to trust that God is able to win the battle they are facing.
2. Take action to renew their vision and passion whenever they feel "sleepy" in their ministry. If they feel tempted to stay back from the battle, as some of the tribes of Israel did, to instead rise up and join in the battle once again.

Your thoughts:

Faith Worth Dying For

by K. Sutter

Hebrews 11:1 & 6 *"Now faith is the assurance of things hoped for, the conviction of things not seen."*
"And without faith it is impossible to please God, because anyone who comes to him must believe that he exists and that he rewards those who earnestly seek him."

So begins Hebrews chapter 11, God's list of Heroes of the Faith. These people of Old Testament times had unswerving confidence in God's character. Each one believed—in spite of impossible circumstances—that God would keep His promises. Rather than responding in unbelief as a result of the things they could see, they responded in faith to the One they could not see. Even if the promises were not fulfilled within their lifetime, they looked beyond, remaining faithful to the very end.

Our frontline worker, Chris, while working to see God's Kingdom come in a very risky situation in a Muslim country, recorded a message on the topic of "Faith" to be listened to by fellow believers. He quoted Thomas Jefferson (the third American President): "Only those who can see the invisible can do the impossible." Chris continued, "Is my life about this—He who is invisible—or is it about what is visible? Will people write something about me one day? If so, my prayer is that they will say, 'By faith he did this for the Lord.' ...faith and fear cannot coexist...."

Shortly after giving his message, Chris was martyred by religious extremists. As with the other heroes in Hebrews 11, Chris did not see his hopes fulfilled. Yet we can say, "Chris, by faith you did this for the Lord." And we can add, "God keeps His promises." One year later, Chris' father Jay said, "God has taken an evil deed and turned it into something good in the advancement of His Kingdom. I have personally participated in and I have heard of conferences, meetings and revivals here and in countries abroad where Chris' work and his ministry have inspired and recommitted believers to the spread of the gospel, the task to which our Lord has called all of us."

Jackie, Chris' wife, said his death has increased her own "passion for the Lord and His work. Even our children have dreams of following in their dad's footsteps." Jackie is actively pursuing their vision for the unreached.

In the land where he died, the Minister of Justice pledged that Chris'"work and legacy will continue. Though we are mourning his death, he has left a lasting impression that will not die."

Of the people mentioned in Hebrews 11 and the people like Chris, Hebrews declares,

"God is not ashamed to be called their God. They are people 'of whom the world was not worthy....'" But God is worthy of their faith. God's purposes will be accomplished. The faithful will see His promises fulfilled, even if they may only see from Heaven.

Personal questions to consider:

1. What in your life is worth dying for?
2. If people write about you in the future, what do you pray they will say?

Pray for the Frontline Workers to:

1. Think about the legacy they hope to leave behind on the mission field.
2. Seek God for wisdom and guidance in the face of extreme danger. Pray for supernatural protection.
Please also pray for Chris' wife and children and the people for whom he gave his life.

Your thoughts:

Peace! Be Still!

by K. Sutter

Mark 4:40   *"He said to His disciples, 'Why are you so afraid? Do you still have no faith?'"*

The disciples were unable to navigate in the storm. Waves poured into the boat. Water came in faster than they could bail it out. They were helpless to stop the increasing water. Before long the boat would sink. To sink in this storm, was to drown.

Back at the stern, Jesus lay sound asleep on a comfortable cushion. How could He remain so uninvolved? Was He unaware of the crisis? Maybe He just did not care. Which of these would have been the greater fear for His disciples: "We're going to drown!" or "Jesus doesn't care about us!"?

Neither were true. Moments later came a radical change. They heard Him speak out a command to the storm, "Peace! Be still!" The next thing they knew, the wind ceased and a great calm settled upon the surface of the water. This awesomely powerful Man onboard turned His face to them, "How can it be that you have no faith in Me? Are you still unable to firmly trust?"

He wanted them to be unafraid and trust Him even in life-threatening situations. The disciples found this difficult. For them, the Gospel Story was still unfolding day by day. They didn't have the whole picture. They were right in the midst of Jesus making history. So far, they had only witnessed a small part of what Jesus would eventually do. They did not know where things were going or how it would all work out. Yet Jesus expected their complete trust.

What does He expect of us? We do have the whole story, from beginning to end, told and retold from four different perspectives; Matthew, Mark, Luke and John. We know these historical accounts of what Jesus said and what He did. We also know our personal stories, our family's stories and our friends' stories of Jesus faithfully bringing peace in the midst of trouble.

To add to it all, we have His Holy Spirit living within us confirming to us that He is trustworthy. He's been trustworthy in the past. He is trustworthy now. Jesus is the same yesterday, today and forever.

When we dedicate ourselves to living for Jesus in the midst of a community which knows nothing about Him, we encounter times of trouble. Troubles take many forms. Some hit like loud, terrible storms—on the frontlines a team and their disciples are threatened by violent persecution. Others creep in quietly—negative thoughts that keep coming to your mind. On the frontlines one begins to think: "These people will never come to Jesus. I am wasting of my life. I should quit and go home."

Will these troubles sink us? Not with Jesus in the boat. As difficult and discouraging as things may become, never doubt—Jesus does care. Do not be afraid. In faith, lift your eyes to see His face and open your ears to hear for His words, "Peace! Be still!"

 Personal questions to consider:

1. What circumstances push you to fearful thoughts?
2. When these kinds of circumstances come again, what do you already know from God's Word and from your own experience that will strengthen your faith and help you find His peace?

 Pray for the Frontline Workers to:

1. Be aware of circumstances that push them to fearful thoughts.
2. When faced with fear: remind themselves of what they know from God's Word and their experiences with Him. Pray they would be strengthened in faith and would find His peace.

 Your thoughts:

Voices Raised

by K. Sutter

Acts 4:23-30   *"On their release, Peter and John went back to their own people and reported all that the chief priests and the elders had said to them. When they heard this, they raised their voices together in prayer to God... 'Now, Lord, consider their threats and enable your servants to speak Your Word with great boldness.'"*

As I write, a Middle Eastern friend and coworker has just been released from prison in North Africa. Sadly his teammate remains locked up.* Their crime: possession of Christian literature. I can only imagine how frightening this has been for them, their families and their team. It is a story not unlike Peter and John's.

Peter and John were imprisoned. Before their release they were threatened by the authorities and commanded to stop speaking or teaching about Jesus. Once freed, Peter and John immediately gathered with fellow believers--the new church. When all had heard their report, together as one, they lifted up their voices to God.

The fact they turned to God and prayed is not unexpected. What they prayed is unexpected. A normal human response might be: "Lord, Thank You for releasing our two brothers. Please stop this from ever happening again. Protect Peter and John. Shield us all. Help us be more careful when we talk to others and guard everything we say. Watch over our safety. Keep us from any harm. Amen."

While this may have been a reasonable prayer, it was not their prayer. Without any mention of protection, they cried out to God for the ability to declare the Gospel fearlessly—with great boldness and to demonstrate His power through signs and wonders. This must have been the prayer God wanted to hear because, "After they prayed, the place where they were meeting was shaken. And they were all filled with the Holy Spirit and spoke the Word of God boldly." (Acts 4:31)

It is little wonder the early church experienced supernatural increase daily. Facing the enemy's threats of violence and imprisonment, they prayed for boldness. They relied upon God to fill them with the Holy Spirit, enabling them to press through to victory. Just as back in their time in Jerusalem, it is similar today in our time among the unreached. The enemy has his plan: "Stop this thing from spreading any further among the people." (Acts 4:17) Threatening circumstances will come, attempting to stop supernatural increase. Let us dare, with voices raised, to ask to be filled with the Holy Spirit so we may press on with freedom, courage and boldness toward supernatural increase.

* Thankfully the second Middle Eastern brother was later released.

Personal questions to consider:

1. What is your prayer when facing the enemy's threats?
2. How might you gather more believers together and pray like the early church for the spread of the Gospel among the unreached?

Pray for the Frontline Workers to:

1. Discern how the enemy is trying to "stop this thing from spreading any further" among their people.
2. Seek the Lord on what He would have them do about it.
Your

Your thoughts:

_____
_____
_____
_____
_____
_____
_____
_____
_____
_____
_____
_____

The Power of Praise

by C. Anderson

Act 16:25 *"About midnight Paul and Silas were praying and singing hymns to God, and the other prisoners were listening to them…"*

Paul and Silas had gone to Philippi at the direction of God. God had spoken clearly to Paul that he should go to Macedonia. They had faithfully shared His Word and signs and wonders had followed that Word. Paul cast out a demon spirit from a girl and what happened? He ends up in trouble. He is beaten, falsely accused and thrown in prison. This isn't the outcome we usually expect when we obey God's direction and move in the power and anointing of His Spirit! Instead of seeing the town come to Christ, he faced anger and attack.

What was the response of Paul and his coworker to these difficulties? They prayed and worshipped. Paul knew the power of coming into the presence of God. When we begin to worship; our doubts, fears and discouragement fall away. Faith for the miraculous rises in our hearts. We turn our eyes on Jesus, and then God is free to work!

Prayer changes things…including us! As we know, when they began to worship, an earthquake came, their chains were loosed and the doors to the prison opened. The jailer came running, ready to kill himself, but Paul stopped him and shared the love of God. That night the jailer and his whole family believed.

As we choose to pray and worship, rather than grumbling and complaining about our difficulties, the power of God is released. Things begin to happen. Our oppressors and those who were against us, start asking questions as they see our witness.

Whatever difficulty you face, choose today to pray and praise. God can turn things around for you. Maybe today will be the day for a key breakthrough!

Personal questions to consider:

1. When you face difficulties, how do you usually respond? Is your first reaction to complain or turn your eyes on Jesus?
2. How do you think about those who give you a hard time? How could you begin to see them as potential people who ask, "What must I do to be saved?"

Pray for the Frontline Workers to:

1. Overcome complaining with thanksgiving and worship.
2. Teach their disciples how to respond to their persecutors and to love their enemies.

Your thoughts:

Aggressive Determination

by K. Sutter

Mark 2:3-5 *"Some men came, bringing to him a paralyzed man, carried by four of them. Since they could not get him to Jesus because of the crowd, they made an opening in the roof above Jesus by digging through it and then lowered the mat the man was lying on. When Jesus saw their faith, He said to the paralyzed man, 'Son, your sins are forgiven.'"*

When Jesus saw their faith, the supernatural took place. Here is a mystery. Jesus fully intended to heal the sick. It was His will and the will of His Father. Yet the active anticipation, expectancy and utter confidence that Jesus would do the supernatural—seemed to be the human spark for it to happen.

These four men and their paralyzed friend were not passive. With aggressive determination they went to Jesus but found the house full. There was no room at the door to even look inside. "We will not give up. We will find a way. We will make a way."

"Get him on the stretcher. Grab the poles. Climb the walls. Pull him up on top. Hold the rope. Lower him down…." With faith in God, they expected Jesus to respond. But what a disruption, what a mess—rubble fell upon people's heads. How embarrassing to be lowered into the crowded house in front of all these upset people. The men took such a risk.

Jesus responds, "My son, your sins are forgiven…get up, take your mat and go home." Their faith was rewarded with transformation both spiritual and physical! Looking down through the roof, they must have shouted: "Oh! Jesus did it! He's walking!" For the rest of their lives these men must have told and retold their amazing story, "Jesus saw our faith and we saw the miraculous!"

May we follow their example of aggressive determination by gathering our faith and doing whatever it takes to see Jesus do the supernatural.

Personal questions to consider:

1. Of the individuals and families you know, who is in desperate need of being brought to Jesus now?
2. What action must be taken and who should help?

Pray for the Frontline Workers to:

1. Identify which individuals and families in their community are in desperate need of being brought to Jesus.
2. Spend time in prayer and ask Jesus what action to take.

Your thoughts:

Miraculous Catch

by C. Anderson

Luke 5:5 *"Simon answered, "Master, we've worked hard all night and haven't caught anything. But because You say so, I will let down the nets."*

Simon was a good fisherman. He had been fishing for many years and he knew how to fish. But this night, he came up empty. His efforts had produced nothing. His wisdom, training, knowledge and experience had failed him. Then he met Jesus. Jesus asked him if He could use his boat to preach to the people. Peter agreed.

After Jesus was finished sharing with the people, He gave Simon some very strange instructions. "Go out into the deep water and put down your nets." Simon had just fished all night. He knew, as everyone knew, that the time to fish was at night, not in the daytime. What did this Teacher and carpenter know about fishing?

Simon expressed his doubt, but then he made a very important decision. He took a risk of faith and obeyed the Master Jesus. He obeyed and did something that made little sense to his natural mind. What was the result of this risky obedience? They got the biggest catch of fish they had ever seen or dreamed of! Their nets filled, both boats filled, and they could barely bring all the fish to shore!

Jesus wants us to be willing to listen to His voice and obey Hm. He is asking us to take risks and step out in faith and obedience to His direction. It is easy after doing ministry for many years on the frontlines, to rely on ones own experience and knowledge, instead of asking Him each day for His direction and leading. Jesus knows how to catch the fish! He knows where we should cast the nets!

If you are working hard but not seeing much fruit, maybe it's time to listen again to the Master and get His fresh direction and leading in how He wants you to work. Maybe He is already speaking to you, but the direction He is giving feels too risky, or too different from what you are used to doing. Let's be willing to do new things in new ways. God wants to fill our boats with fish and bring a greater fruitfulness in our work than we have ever dreamed of!

Personal questions to consider:

1. When do you find it easy to listen for God's specific direction?
2. When is it more difficult for you to listen to God?

Pray for the Frontline Workers to:

1. Remember when the Holy Spirit led them to do something unusual, new or different in their ministry and then reflect upon what happened as they obeyed Him.
2. Find ways to frequently listen for God's direction.

Your thoughts:

_____

_____

_____

_____

_____

_____

_____

_____

_____

_____

_____

DAY
20

The Power of Perspective

by C. Anderson

Numbers 13:30 *"Then Caleb silenced the people before Moses and said, "We should go up and take possession of the land, for we can certainly do it.""*

What was it that made Caleb different from the rest of the spies? They had gone on the same trip, seen the same things. But they came back with very different perspectives. Ten of the spies came back saying "it does flow with milk and honey! Here is its fruit. But the people who live there are powerful…" It is good, but…. They saw the dream and the vision, they saw the good things available to them. But they also saw the obstacles, difficulties and how powerful and great was their enemy. And this is where they chose to focus their attention.

Caleb was different. He had a confidence, a faith, that with God's help they could "certainly do it." He urged them to go up and take possession of the promise God had given. He was not ignorant of the obstacles and difficulties, but he refused to let those things make him stop moving forward. "Let's go! Let's do it!" This was his attitude.

Perspective (how we see things) is everything. Our perspective will determine our attitudes and our actions. Sometimes when I think about church planting movements and the task of seeing communities and peoples transformed, I am tempted to focus on the difficulties. There are times when I feel overwhelmed by all the impossibilities. Sometimes the giants look so big to me.

I want to be like Caleb though. I want to focus on God; His ability and His promise. I want to be someone who says "Let's go up and take possession! We can certainly do it!" Let's go bless these unreached peoples and see His Kingdom come among them. God has promised it! It is our inheritance to claim and ask God for the nations for His glory. Let's go up. We can do it. Whether on the frontlines or on the home-front, let's stir up our faith in Him and what He has promised us. God is able. He can give us movements! He can bring hope; blessing and transformation to peoples and nations.

Personal questions to consider:

1. Do you tend to be more like Caleb or more like the other spies? Do you usually see the positive or negative in situations?
2. How could you gain a perspective that is more like Caleb's?

Pray for the Frontline Workers to:

1. Reflect upon whether they tend to be like Caleb or like the other spies—seeing more of the positive or more of the negative.
2. Consider what difficulties or obstacles they have faced lately and recognize if they have caused them to feel small and weak. Ask God to give them a perspective like Caleb's once again.

Your thoughts:

Revealed to Children

by K. Sutter

Luke 10:17 & 21 *"The seventy-two returned.... At that time Jesus, full of joy through the Holy Spirit, said, 'I praise You, Father, Lord of heaven and earth, because You have hidden these things from the wise and learned, and revealed them to little children. Yes, Father, for this is what You were pleased to do.'"*

Luke 8 starts with Jesus teaching about bearing fruit. He goes on to demonstrate by casting out demons, healing the sick and even raising the dead. As always, Jesus bore supernatural fruit.

Luke 9 starts with Jesus sending out the Twelve, two-by-two, proclaiming the Kingdom of God and healing the sick. The Apostles bore supernatural fruit.

Luke 10 starts with Jesus sending 72 other disciples proclaiming the Kingdom of God and healing the sick. The seventy-two bore supernatural fruit.

As the 72 returned, Jesus was full of joy. He turned to the Apostles and privately said, "Blessed are the eyes that see what you see. For I tell you that many prophets and kings wanted to see what you see but did not see it, and to hear what you hear but did not hear it."

Here is one of the amazing things the Apostles had just witnessed with their own eyes and ears—Jesus multiplying workers for His Kingdom. But rather than choosing workers from among the "wise and learned," He chose common, everyday people with faith like little children.

In Delhi, I was teaching on how to start self-multiplying fellowships among the unreached. Many of our church planters from across North India gathered. During a break I stood outside sipping chai with a friend. Looking to his left he said, "See the brother over there? When he came to Jesus he was a 'coolie.' His job was carrying heavy loads of brick on his back, up and down steep Himalayan paths for building projects. With his new love for Jesus, he dedicated himself to spread the Gospel among Nepali people."

My friend continued, "In spite of being unable to read or write he's already started seven simple churches. He is one of our most fruitful coworkers!" I can almost hear Jesus with a joyful laugh crying out, "I thank You Father!" God is not primarily looking for brilliant, highly educated, well-financed, ordained "superstars." Above all, He wants people with child-like faith. When a little boy knows he is loved by his father he wants to be with him. When a little girl knows she is loved by her father, she happily runs up to ask, "What are you doing? Can I help?" With hearts of love, they please their father, eager to do what he says.

Do you know you are unconditionally loved by your Heavenly Father? Do you long to be with Him? Are you eager to join Him as He gathers the Harvest? Are you careful to do whatever He says? Whoever answers yes, yes, yes, yes is qualified to proclaim the Kingdom, heal the sick and celebrate with joy!

Personal questions to consider:

1. How confident are you of your Heavenly Father's love for you?
2. What are you doing this week to spread the blessings of His Kingdom?

Pray for the Frontline Workers to:

1. Look at their disciples and decide who among them have the qualifications mentioned above.
2. Equip, multiply and send workers like Jesus did.

Your thoughts:

Consecrate Yourselves

by C. Anderson

Joshua 3:5 *"Joshua told the people, 'Consecrate yourselves, for tomorrow the Lord will do amazing things among you.'"*

Joshua spoke these words just before the Israelites crossed the Jordan, entered the promised land and headed for the battle at Jericho. "Consecrate yourselves" he said. "God is about to do something big. Tomorrow you will see amazing things. Get yourselves ready." This instruction to consecrate or make themselves holy, was commonly given in the Bible. Before a great battle, or a forward advance, God often spoke to the Israelites telling them to make themselves holy, to cleanse their homes, bodies and lives.

As we look at the things which God has declared He wants to do among the unreached, these words of Joshua seem fitting for us to consider. God is about to do amazing things among us. He is going to bring about a supernatural increase in the harvest. He is about to bring great breakthroughs. We will see movements among the unreached like we have never seen before.

As we look forward in faith, let's take time to "consecrate ourselves." Consecration means being set apart, being holy. Leviticus 20:7-8 says "Consecrate yourselves and be holy, because I am the Lord your God. Keep My decrees and follow them. I am the Lord who makes you holy."

Are there things in our lives, relationships or homes, that we need to allow God to come and cleanse? Have we been drawing pleasure from the things of the world instead of from God? Have we given into sinful habits or thoughts? Are we being entertained by ungodly things like certain books, TV, internet, phone messages, chat, or movies that fill our minds with the ways and patterns of the world?

God calls us to holiness and to living separately from the world. Our source of joy, contentment, and pleasure should first of all be Him…being in His presence, His Word, worship, fellowship. Maybe we need to get rid of some things from our lives or homes. Maybe we need to stop watching certain things. Let's consecrate ourselves, return to holiness and being set apart. Tomorrow God will do amazing things among us!

Personal questions to consider:

1. When are you tempted to draw pleasure from things that are ungodly or to give into sinful patterns?
2. How will you repent, turn from those things and consecrate yourself once again?

Pray for the Frontline Workers to:

1. Avoid bad habits or poor use of time when faced with boredom, discouragement or restlessness.
2. "Drink in" from God as their source when they are tempted with unhealthy, worldly pleasures.

Your thoughts:

_____
_____
_____
_____
_____
_____
_____
_____
_____
_____
_____
_____
_____

Every Nation?

by K. Sutter

Revelation 7:9 *"After this I looked, and there before me was a great multitude that no one could count, from every nation, tribe, people and language, standing before the throne and before the Lamb. They were wearing white robes and were holding palm branches in their hands."*

Every nation, tribe, people? Yes, we want to believe it but often the obstacles seem immovable.

At a Conference On Frontier Missions in the late 1980s, a speaker told us of one of the largest and most difficult people groups to reach—the Uzbeks. Their land, Uzbekistan, was locked up within Communist USSR. Outsiders were forbidden to enter this Muslim country.

Every nation? All tribes and people groups? Every...all...including the Uzbeks? Yes, every. Within two years of hearing about the Uzbeks, I stood in front of our television watching the Berlin Wall—the symbol of Communism's Iron Curtain" being broken down. The world was shocked! The USSR opened to the world. Suddenly, unexpectedly a way was paved to the Uzbeks. Shortly thereafter, scores of missionaries arrived in Uzbekistan. They set about learning the language and culture; building friendships and talking about Jesus.

Eventually Uzbeks opened their hearts and believed the Good News. Lives were transformed, fellowships established and local elders trained and commissioned. What once seemed unattainable became reality. Uzbek people were loving and obeying Jesus and sharing the Gospel with others.

Not long ago, the government tried to bring the growing movement to a halt by forcing all missionaries out and intensifying persecution of the Uzbek church. Despite this new obstacle, the local believers continue to remain strong and press on toward God's purposes for their people and their land.

As I look back over these years my heart is full of gratitude that God accomplished what once seemed so impossible. Yes there will be Uzbeks in the midst of that multitude John saw—many of them! How will God draw in the remaining thousands of unreached tribes and nations? It's not up to us to figure it out ourselves. He has His ways. Between now and then, let's pray in faith—He's done it before, He'll do it again—remaining ever available to do the part He gives us to do.

Personal questions to consider:

1. What obstacle seems immovable right now?
2. What would you do if suddenly that obstacle vanished?

Pray for the Frontline Workers to:

Ask themselves the same two questions you answered:
1. What obstacle seems immovable to us right now?
2. What would we do if suddenly that obstacle vanished?

Your thoughts:

DAY 24

Go in the Strength You Have

by C. Anderson

Judges 6:14 *"The Lord turned to him and said, 'Go in the strength you have and save Israel out of Midian's hand. Am I not sending you?'"*

God often chooses weak people to accomplish His great victories. When the Angel of the Lord appeared to Gideon He called him a "mighty warrior." Gideon responded saying, "I am from the weakest clan and the least in my family." The Lord answered him, assuring him that He would be with him.

That still didn't convince him fully. Gideon asked the Angel of the Lord for a sign. The Angel responded by touching His staff to Gideon's offering. It burst into flames. Then he knew. This was God who was calling him and he got ready to obey.

Gideon's faith was not in himself. He knew his weaknesses and that he was not worthy. But once he knew God was with him, he began to believe, obey and take action. We are asking God for impossible things. We believe Him for miracles; for the transformation of individuals, families, communities and people groups. Only God can do that! And He has chosen us to be a part of that miracle!

In faith let us stand with our frontline workers as they would declare: "Like Gideon, we 'go in the strength we have' to bring His salvation to the people to whom God has called us. We go, not with faith in ourselves, but faith in a Mighty God who says 'Am I not sending you?'"

Personal questions to consider:

1. When, if ever, do you feel weak and small compared to the tasks God has given you?
2. What "strength" do you already have that you can begin to move in, knowing God has called you and is with you?

Pray for the Frontline Workers to:

1. Consider when, if ever, they feel weak and small compared to the task of reaching an unreached people group or planting a movement of reproducing fellowships.
2. Remind themselves of any signs or confirmations God gave when He chose them for this task and calling.

Your thoughts:

_____

_____

_____

_____

_____

_____

_____

_____

_____

_____

_____

_____

God Decreases Gideon

by C. Anderson

Judges 7:2-3   *"You have too many men for me to deliver Midian into their hands. In order that Israel may not boast against Me that her own strength has saved her...anyone who trembles with fear may turn back..."*

Do you ever feel like things are getting worse, not better? Gideon certainly must have. He blew the trumpet in the power of the Holy Spirit and summoned his troops to war. 32,000 people gathered and were ready to do battle. Then God said "You have too many men." God reduced his army first to 10,000 and then down to 300. Talk about your team members quitting on you!

I wonder about those 300 men. What were they like? They followed Gideon into battle with the odds against them. They were filled with faith in a God who could do the miraculous, through only a few committed people. And He did! God used only 300 to defeat a massive army and to bring deliverance to the people of Israel.

It isn't about how many people we have on the field, or how much support they have, or about their resources or skills. God wants to receive the glory when church planting movements start. Sometimes, He allows us to lose people or resources, so we will truly look to Him in faith to do what only He can do through what remains.

Personal questions to consider:

1. In what ways have you experienced a decrease in your "natural ability"?
2. How might God turn this decrease around and use it to bring about an increase in your fruitfulness?

Pray for the Frontline Workers to:

1. See any ways they have experienced a decrease in their "natural abilities" to move their ministry toward growth and expansion.
2. Ask themselves, "How could this decrease provide an opportunity for us to involve the local believers to a greater extent?"

Your thoughts:

Astonished by Love

by K. Sutter

Acts 4:19-20 *"But Peter and John replied, 'Which is right in God's eyes: to listen to you, or to Him? You be the judges! As for us, we cannot help speaking about what we have seen and heard.'"*

Peter and John met a crippled beggar on their way to the temple. They responded to his need just like their Master would have done. In moments he was walking and leaping and praising God! As a crowd of amazed people gathered, Peter saw a perfect chance to speak out for Jesus. All this upset the religious authorities who had the two disciples tossed into jail.

After an uncomfortable night in the Jerusalem cell, Peter and John next came face to face with the intimidating high priest, rulers, elders and teachers. The authorities were certain their threats would silence the disciples. Despite this pressure, the disciples made it clear—they would listen to God and obey Him.

Peter and John chose to obey God's commands rather than human commands. Jesus taught us the greatest commandment: "Love God and love your neighbor as you love yourself." Do this always. You and the world around you will be changed! Simple obedience to this command takes care of everything.

The enemy's strategy for victory: fear. God's strategy for victory: love.

One of our church planters in a Muslim country tells of a local believer and his simple obedience to love God and others…even his enemy. Abdul has boldness similar to Peter and John. He often shares the Gospel with the police and radical Muslims. Not long ago, a group threatened to burn down his house and harm his daughters. One day, as he drove his car, he saw one of the men who threatened him walking down the street. He sensed the Lord speaking, "Go back. Pick him up. Bring him where he needs to go." He battled the thought briefly, but then turned his car around. He stopped and offered his enemy a ride. The man was shocked but climbed in.

As Abdul drove he asked his passenger about his work. The man replied, "I do not have a job." Abdul had just heard about a job opening. He asked the man if he wanted to go find out about it. Abdul talked with the owner of the business and the man was offered the job right on the spot.

His "enemy" thanked him for helping and apologized for the things he had said and threatened to do. He went on to say, "Abdul you are a great man and I see this even more through your actions today."

Listening to God, Peter, John and Abdul had an impact on people: "…they were astonished and they took note that these men had been with Jesus." (Acts 4:13) Let this be true of us all as we listen to the Voice of Love. God is free to bless us with supernatural increase when we simply obey His Great Command.

Personal questions to consider:

1. Abdul knew and obeyed Jesus' command to love his enemy. How well do you know and obey Jesus' commands?
2. Abdul sensed the Lord speak to him. When was the last time you heard God's voice and obeyed?

Pray for the Frontline Workers to:

1. Evaluate how well their disciples know and obey Jesus' commands.
2. Ask their disciples about the last time they heard God's voice and obeyed.

Your thoughts:

DAY 27

Increase and Move Out

by C. Anderson

Deuteronomy 1:11 & 21 *"May the Lord, the God of your fathers increase you a thousand times and bless you as he has promised!" "See the Lord your God has given you the land. Go up and take possession of it as the Lord, the God of your fathers, told you. Do not be afraid; do not be discouraged."*

Moses wanted to see the Israelites continue to increase and grow. They had already grown a lot! They had become so large that they now needed many more leaders. Growth is good, but it means we have to delegate. Raising new leaders is a lot of work! In spite of this, we hear Moses asking God to increase them a thousand times more!

I think if Moses looked at the work of church planting among the unreached, he might say something similar. It is time to see a release of workers and leaders like we have never seen. Ten- fold increase seems small compared to the thousand times increase Moses requested!

In order for that increase to come, some things had to happen. First, as we have seen, more leaders had to be appointed. Second, they had to move out in new things. Deut 1:6 says "You have stayed long enough at this mountain." Later it says "Go in and take possession…." God is calling us to leave the mountain where we are comfortable, and move out into new and greater things. Hanging on to old ways, forms or experiences keep us from inheriting the promised land ahead. Third, they had to move forward in faith. They needed to resist fear and discouragement and take the land. They had to put their trust firmly on God's character and promises.

Sadly, the children of Israel failed the test. They didn't go forward in faith. Their fear to kept them back. They lost their inheritance and wandered in the wilderness for forty years. Only Caleb and Joshua entered in. Later, the rest believed. But it was too late. They obeyed God but were defeated because God's blessing had lifted and was no longer with them.

I don't want to be too late in trusting God! I sometimes struggle with fears, discouragement and doubts. But God calls us to put our hope and trust in Him! He is the one who called us to take the land! God himself goes before you to fight for you.

Personal questions to consider:

1. What fears or discouragements have you faced in the last six months? To what extent have those fears or disappointments shaken your trust in God's promise or character?
2. How can you reaffirm your trust and make your faith more "active" today?

Pray for the Frontline Workers to:

1. Recall specific promises God Himself has given them as they have worked with Him among the unreached.
2. Stimulate and stir up their faith in God's promises.

Your thoughts:

_____

_____

_____

_____

_____

_____

_____

_____

_____

_____

_____

_____

_____

DAY 28

Hold on to Hope

by C. Anderson

Hebrews 10:23 *"Let us hold unswervingly to the hope we profess, for He who promised is faithful."*

Hebrews chapter ten and eleven are both wonderful faith chapters in the Bible. Chapter 10 verse 22 speaks of how we need to draw near to God with sincere hearts and with full assurance of faith. It also reminds us of the importance of being cleansed and our guilty conscience washed clean.

This is a reminder for us of the importance of remaining close to God and of keeping our hearts clean before Him, if we want to move in supernatural faith. A dirty heart causes distance in our relationship with God and with others. As we work in His service, we face various conflicts, problems and stresses. It's easy to take offense. It's easy to give in to temptations. And we all do fail from time to time.

These verses remind us that at those times, we need to draw near to God and be cleansed. Instead of running from Him and letting those sins and problems make our relationship with God feel distant, we must run to Him for His help and cleansing.

Another emphasis of these verses comes in verse 23 quoted above. It tells us to "hold unswervingly" or to hold tight to the hope we profess. This verse always reminds me of a picture from my childhood. We had a small pet dog that liked to play with us. We would give the dog a cloth and the dog would bite it and refuse to let go. We could even pick the dog up off the ground by lifting the cloth and it would hold on tight with its teeth. That is what this passage is talking about.

Hold on tight to your hope! Don't let go of faith that God is going to do something great among Muslim, Hindu and Buddhist peoples…those who have never heard the Good News about Jesus! Be like that dog, that wouldn't let go, no matter what! Sometimes the devil or circumstances might even pick you up off the ground…but you are holding on to the promises of God. Refuse to let go! God is going to answer because, as this verse says, "He who promised is faithful." In faith, hold on tight to the dreams and vision God has put in your heart.

Personal questions to consider:

1. How are you doing at "drawing near" to God?
2. In your faith, how much are you like that dog, refusing to let go?

Pray for the Frontline Workers to:

1. Avoid allowing the enemy to rob them of faith and confidence in God.
2. Hold on "doggedly" to the promise God has given.

Your thoughts:

DAY
29

Receive Power

by K. Sutter

Acts 1:8   *"But you will receive power when the Holy Spirit comes on you; and you will be My witnesses in Jerusalem, and in all Judea and Samaria, and to the ends of the earth."*

As Jesus gathered with His disciples, He commanded them not to leave Jerusalem but to wait. He told them, "You will be baptized in the Holy Spirit not many days from now." Even after spending time with the resurrected Lord Jesus, they were still not ready to start the global supernatural spread of the Gospel. Another world-changing event was about to occur.

God was preparing to draw even closer to His people. In the past, the disciples knew God from a distance: He dwelt within the Temple in Jerusalem. Now at this point, the disciples knew God by their side: He dwelt within His Son Jesus. In the near future, they would know God from the very closest place: He would dwell within them.

In an upper room 120 men and women waited with simple confidence. They fully trusted that Jesus would fulfill His promise of power to be His witnesses. "Suddenly a sound like the blowing of a violent wind came from heaven and filled the whole house where they were sitting. They saw what seemed to be tongues of fire that separated and came to rest on each of them. All of them were filled with the Holy Spirit and began to speak in other tongues as the Spirit enabled them."

The Church came to Life! It was the birthday of the Church, Pentecost. Before the end of that day, 3,000 people were baptized and added. The power of the Holy Spirit launched a revolutionary spiritual movement. Each believer received power to be like Jesus. Believers were released into mental, moral and spiritual transformation—"inner signs and wonders." They were released into "outer signs and wonders," such as healing the sick, casting our demons and prophecy.

They received power to love God and love their neighbors, power to produce fruit of the Spirit and power to be His witnesses. Over ten times in the Book of Acts, Luke carefully notes the incredible numerical growth of the newly born church. They had no formal structure. They simply gathered from house to house. Motivated by love and obedience to Jesus, the early believers multiplied their numbers by sharing the Good News everywhere with everyone throughout Jerusalem.

The blessings of God's Kingdom which poured out in Jerusalem (the City of the Great

King) will spread to the ends of the earth. We've been called to be part of finishing this supernatural task. We've been given the power for supernatural increase. Listen to Jesus and do what He says. He's not far, the very Spirit of Jesus dwells within us!

 Personal questions to consider:

1. Where in your personal life or ministry do you need more power?
2. What can you do to draw upon the power of the Holy Spirit?

 Pray for the Frontline Workers to:

Ask themselves the same two questions you answered:
1. Where in my personal life or ministry do I need more power?
2. What can I do to draw upon the power of the Holy Spirit?

Your thoughts:

_____

_____

_____

_____

_____

_____

_____

_____

_____

_____

_____

The Spirit Leads the Way

by K. Sutter

Acts 13:2-3 *"While they were worshiping the Lord and fasting, the Holy Spirit said, 'Set apart for me Barnabas and Saul for the work to which I have called them.' So after they had fasted and prayed, they placed their hands on them and sent them off."*

The Holy Spirit leads. He mobilizes, directs and empowers His people to obey the Great Commandment and Great Commission with passion and joy. We see Him in the Book of Acts and in history (His story).

See the Holy Spirit's work in the newborn Church: "They broke bread in their homes and ate together with glad and sincere hearts, praising God and enjoying the favor of all the people. And the Lord added to their number daily those who were being saved." (Acts 2:46-47) They loved God, they loved one another. Love spilled over upon their neighbors.

As the Holy Spirit filled up and flowed out of believers, they became like powerful magnets pulling many into the Kingdom. Even Pharisees and other religious leaders couldn't resist and turned to Jesus. Growth was so rapid, non-believing leaders got desperate. Intense persecution arose. Stephen was martyred.

Most believers fled. They left Jerusalem, but they did not leave the Holy Spirit. Dwelling within, He gave power to be His witnesses…in all Judea and Samaria. In Antioch some reached out cross-culturally to Greeks. Unexpectedly, many Greeks believed! Barnabas was sent from Jerusalem to help. "He was a good man, full of the Holy Spirit and faith, and a great number of people were brought to the Lord." (Acts 11:24) As numbers grew, Barnabas went to get help from Saul (Paul). Saul had also been "filled with the Holy Spirit." (Acts 9:17) For a year the two taught the church in Antioch.

The Spirit was still busy mobilizing His people for the further spread of the Good News. In a time of worship in Antioch He spoke: "Set apart for Me Barnabas and Saul for the work to which I have called them." (Acts 13:2) The Holy Spirit maintained the lead role as seen in the rest of the chapter:

"So, being sent out by the Holy Spirit, they went…." (Acts 13:4)

"Then Saul, who was also called Paul, filled with the Holy Spirit…." (Acts 13:9)

"The word of the Lord spread through the whole region…and the disciples were filled with joy and with the Holy Spirit." (Acts 13:49 & 52)

The Holy Spirit continues to fill, empower and lead His people today to obey the Great Commandment and to bring the Great Commission to completion. May we be so full that there is no room for self-centeredness, unbelief or fear. Let's rely upon God to fill each one of us from within—with a Supernatural Increase of the Holy Spirit. May we be so full inside that God will be free to use us to bring Supernatural Increase outside…"to the ends of the earth."

 Personal questions to consider:

1. How convinced are you that Holy Spirit—the Spirit of Jesus—will lead the way to Supernatural Increase?
2. How committed are you to follow Him wherever He leads? How willing are you to do whatever He says to help complete of the Great Commission?

 Pray for the Frontline Workers to:

1. Evaluate their level of confidence that their church planting plans are aligned with the Holy Spirit's plans.
2. Realize that while the leaders in Antioch were "worshiping the Lord and fasting," the Holy Spirit spoke and revealed His instructions and multiplication was about to happen. Pray that they ask themselves, "Under what circumstances do we and our team hear from the Holy Spirit? How committed are we to follow Him wherever He leads? How committed are we to do whatever He says for this people group to be reached?"

 Your thoughts:

Enjoyed this book?

Write a short review!

We hope you have enjoyed this devotional and your faith has grown!

We would greatly appreciate if you would take 2 or 3 minutes to write a short review of the book on Amazon for us. We want to see many more people encouraged by these devotionals.

Would you do that please?

Thanks so much!

As a thankyou, if you contact us via **http://dmmsfrontiermissions.com** and let us know you've written a review, we will send you a free copy of our next e-book.

Concluding Thoughts

One dictionary (Mirriam-Webster) gives us this definition of hope- "to cherish a desire with anticipation." Seeing the release of hundreds of church planting movements among the unreached is definitely a desire that I cherish. I look forward with great faith and anticipation at the coming years. It's my prayer that God has used this book to build your faith and hope for a supernatural harvest as well. Let's press on. Let's believe and let's ask. Let's pray and let's work. He is with us and He will do as He has promised. Nothing can stop His purposes from being fulfilled.
Ps 138:8
Till His Kingdom comes -

C. Anderson

Our hearts' desire is to see the multiplication of Jesus-Centered fellowships spreading the blessings of God's Kingdom within their families, among their neighbors and throughout the nations. We plant these seeds of the Kingdom in faith.
Jesus said, "This is what the Kingdom of God is like. A man scatters seed on the ground. Night and day, whether he sleeps or gets up, the seed sprouts and grows, though he does not know how. All by itself the soil produces grain— first the stalk, then the head, then the full kernel in the head. As soon as the grain is ripe, he puts the sickle to it, because the harvest has come." (Mark 4:26-29)

Like this farmer, we faithfully do our part of the work, but the life that springs forth is God's work. How He brings new life, we don't know. Even while we sleep, He is bringing life. The Apostle Paul, our role model in cross-cultural church planting, knew this truth well and wrote, "I planted the seed, Apollos watered it, but God made it grow." (I Corinthians 3:6)

"Oh, Lord Jesus, we plant with hope for a great harvest. With all the faith we have, we ask You to bring growth, to bring Life. Your Kingdom come!"

K. Sutter

What is a (CPM) *Church Planting Movement* or a (DMM) *Disciple Making Movement?*

This booklet has often used the term "Church Planting Movement." The terms CPM and DMM are basically interchangeable. There are various definitions and understandings of a CPM/DMM. Following are several definitions by leading writers and teachers of CPMs and DMMs.

D. Garrison, IMB:

A definition for Church Planting Movements: "a rapid multiplication of indigenous churches, planting churches that sweeps through a people group or population segment."

D. Watson, New Generations:

To see a CPM, the equipping of leadership is critical. Our definition of leadership includes reproduction of leaders. A leader makes more leaders regularly, and…
To see a CPM, the obedience-based discipleship of all people is essential. Our definition of a disciple includes obedience to Jesus and the reproduction of disciples. An obedient disciple makes more disciples regularly, and…
To see a CPM, Bible story/study groups reproduce regularly, and…
To see a CPM, churches reproduce regularly, and…
To see a CPM, church members are ministering to their communities, and the Kingdom of God is expanding from individual to individual, family to family, community to community, city to city, and nation to nation.

YWAM-Frontier Missions:

Our goal is never only to plant one church. We want to start that groups of Jesus followers (disciples) that then start other groups of disciples growing into movements of disciples. Everything we do should lead to multiplication. Apostolic teams should carefully evaluate their strategies and ways of working to make sure they are reproducible. We avoid doing things that have proven to hinder multiplication, such as building church buildings, paying local pastors or elders, or bringing in a lot of foreign finances and forms.

CPMs or DMMs are fast growing, indigenous movements of obedient Jesus followers. In these movements, disciples gather themselves into groups that we often call churches. These groups multiply and start more groups. A DMM/CPM is a supernatural move of God's Spirit sweeping through an unreached people group where thousands of lives are transformed as people enter God's Kingdom and become part of His family.

May God grant us the joy of seeing many, many DMMs take place among the unreached in these days!

Made in the USA
Monee, IL
21 July 2021